This book belongs to

Avyan

ANGRY earth

POWERFUL EARTHQUAKES

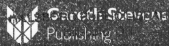

By Greg Roza

Gareth Stevens Publishing

Please visit our website, www.garethstevens.com. For a free color catalog of all our high-quality books, call toll free 1-800-542-2595 or fax 1-877-542-2596.

Library of Congress Cataloging-in-Publication Data

Roza, Greg.
Powerful earthquakes / Greg Roza.
   p. cm. — (Angry Earth)
Includes index.
ISBN 978-1-4339-6547-0 (pbk.)
ISBN 978-1-4339-6548-7 (6-pack)
ISBN 978-1-4339-6545-6 (library binding)
1. Earthquakes—Juvenile literature. I. Title.
QE521.3.R697 2012
551.22—dc23

                                      2011026593

First Edition

Published in 2012 by
Gareth Stevens Publishing
111 East 14th Street, Suite 349
New York, NY 10003

Copyright © 2012 Gareth Stevens Publishing

Designer: Katelyn E. Reynolds
Editor: Therese Shea

Photo credits: Cover, p. 1 Code Red/Collection Mix: Subjects/Getty Images; (cover, pp. 1, 3-32 text/image box graphic) iStockphoto.com; p. 4 Kiyoshi Ota/Getty Images; pp. 5, 8, 9, 13 (inset) Thinkstock.com; pp. 6, 10, 17, (cover, pp. 1, 3-32 background and newspaper graphics) Shutterstock.com; pp. 7 (both), 8 (inset) Dorling Kindersley/Getty Images; p. 11 (inset) Luciano Corbella/Dorling Kindersley/Getty Images; p. 11 James Balog/ Stone/Getty Images; p. 13 Romeo Gacad/AFP/Getty Images; p. 15 DAJ/Getty Images; p. 16 (inset) Tao Chuan Yeh/AFP/Getty Images; p. 16 Deborah Davis/Stone/Getty Images; p. 19 (inset) Pedro Armestre/AFP/Getty Images; p. 19 Jewel Samad/AFP/Getty Images; p. 20 Arnold Genthe/Getty Images; p. 21 (inset) Courtesy of the U.S. Geological Survey; p. 21 Hulton Archive/Getty Images; p. 22 Mike Dunning/Dorling Kindersley/Getty Images; p. 23 (inset) Frederic Dupoux/Getty Images; p. 23 Juan Barreto/AFP/Getty Images; p. 24 DigitalGlobe via Getty Images; p. 25 The Asahi Shimbun via Getty Images; p. 27 (inset) Spencer Platt/Getty Images; p. 27 Nicolas Asfouri/AFP/Getty Images; pp. 28-29 David McNew/Getty Images.

Printed in the United States of America

CPSIA compliance information: Batch #CW12GS: For further information contact Gareth Stevens, New York, New York at 1-800-542-2595.

CONTENTS

Words in the glossary appear in **bold** type the first time they are used in the text.

ALL SHOOK UP!

An earthquake is a shaking of the ground due to the sudden movement of rocks beneath Earth's surface. A quake can last for a few seconds, or it can last several minutes. It might be a light rumble that you barely notice, or furniture can move and objects can fall off walls and shelves. More seriously, the ground can crack open and buildings can **topple**.

Every year, earthquakes affect people around the world. Strong quakes destroy property and claim lives. Although scientists try to **predict** where and when they'll happen, it's not easy. Knowing what to do during a quake will help you stay alive.

2008 earthquake, Japan

The Shaanxi Earthquake

The deadliest earthquake on record occurred in Shaanxi, China, in 1556. About 830,000 people died. At that time, many people in the region lived in man-made caves cut into cliffs. Most of these dwellings were destroyed. The quake opened up giant cracks in the ground and started **landslides** that killed many people.

Some buildings can withstand an earthquake's rumbling while others fall apart. In this photo, the building on the right crumbled while the one on the left remained standing.

EARTH'S CRUST

Earth's outer layer is called the crust. This rock shell ranges from about 3 to 30 miles (4.8 to 48 km) thick. The crust is the top part of a larger layer called the lithosphere. This layer is made of numerous large sections called plates. Earth's plates fit together like puzzle pieces.

The lithosphere "floats" on a layer of soft, hot rock. The plates can "drift" away from each other, leaving gaps. They can also push against each other, slide past one another, or slide under or over each other. These movements create tremendous pressure between the plates.

Continental Drift

Earth's continents have been drifting for a long time. **Geologists** think that Earth's land was grouped into one "supercontinent" called Pangaea about 225 million years ago. It took millions of years for the plates making up the supercontinent to drift apart, in time forming the seven continents we know today.

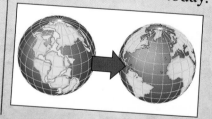

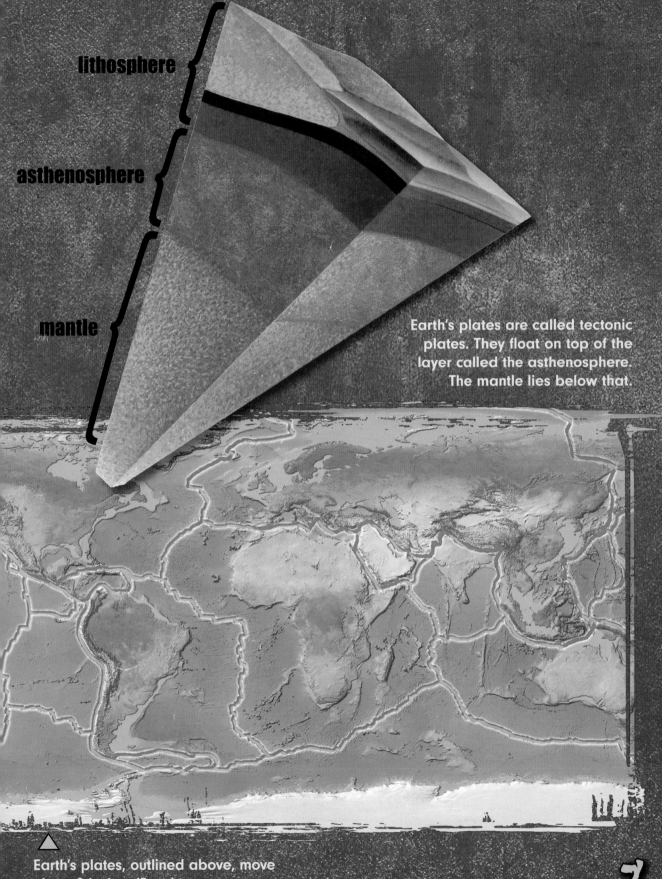

lithosphere

asthenosphere

mantle

Earth's plates are called tectonic plates. They float on top of the layer called the asthenosphere. The mantle lies below that.

Earth's plates, outlined above, move about 2 inches (5 cm) a year.

The Himalayas, shown here, formed between 40 and 50 million years ago when the Indian Plate met the Eurasian Plate. These mountains are still rising as the plates continue to push against each other.

Have you ever tried to stop someone bigger from getting past you? It probably wasn't easy. Earth's plates are very big, and they don't want to stop moving. Two plates create a lot of force when they crash into each other, slide past each other, or slide over or under each other.

Different things can happen where two plates meet. One may slide under the other. Sometimes plates fold under the pressure, rising up to make mountains. These movements don't happen quickly. Pressure builds up between plates over hundreds of years. When two plates suddenly slip and release this pressure, the energy let loose causes an earthquake.

Volcanoes!

Volcanoes form when liquid rock from the mantle rises to Earth's surface. That can happen when one plate slides under another. The sinking plate carries with it water that the heat inside Earth causes to boil, which melts rock that rises to the surface.

A BREAK IN THE CRUST

A fault is a fracture, or break, in Earth's crust. A fault occurs when two sections of crust slip and move by each other. The boundaries between plates are faults. Faults can also form farther away from these boundaries.

There are three main kinds of faults. A normal fault occurs when two blocks of Earth's crust move away from each other. A **reverse** fault occurs when two blocks move toward each other. Both normal and reverse faults result in one block raising up higher than the other. A strike-slip fault occurs when two blocks move **horizontally** in opposite directions.

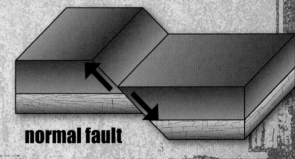

normal fault

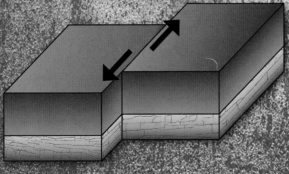

strike-slip fault

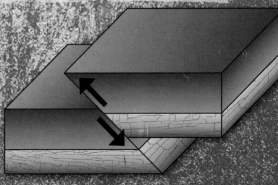

reverse fault

San Andreas Fault

The Pacific Plate and the North American Plate meet to form a strike-slip fault that runs through the state of California. The San Andreas fault is about 800 miles (1,287 km) long. Major earthquakes occur along this fault once every 150 to 200 years.

San Andreas fault

◁ People who live on or near faults often experience the most powerful earthquakes.

RIDE THE WAVE!

During an earthquake, the pressure between two plates is released suddenly. This sends out vibrations, or waves of energy, in all directions. Geologists call these vibrations seismic waves. There are two kinds of seismic waves.

Body waves move from the fault slip toward Earth's surface. Primary body waves (or P waves) move the fastest. They travel through land and water, pushing and pulling as they go. Secondary body waves (or S waves) are slower. They can't travel through water. They move from side to side.

Surface waves travel across Earth's surface. They cause the most **damage** because they move the ground up and down and side to side.

What Is Seismology?

Seismology is the study of seismic waves. Scientists called seismologists use seismic waves to **calculate** the earthquake's focus, or the point where it began. They also calculate the **magnitude** of earthquakes. Someday soon, seismologists hope to be able to predict earthquakes before they happen.

A tool called a seismograph is used
to record and measure the vibrations
caused by earthquakes.

13

QUAKE POWER

Earthquakes can be so strong they change the way Earth looks. They can change a river's course, create valleys, and raise mountains. They can have harmful effects on the places where people live. Strong earthquakes can damage or destroy property. They can injure or kill people and animals.

Earthquake damage depends on several things. An earthquake's magnitude plays a large role in the amount of **destruction** it causes. The farther away from an earthquake's focus, the weaker the **tremors** will be. The type of soil or rock where an earthquake hits also has an effect on how much damage it causes.

Measuring Earthquakes

Scientists use several scales to measure the magnitude of earthquakes. The most common one is called the Richter scale. Each whole number in the Richter scale represents a magnitude 10 times more powerful than the whole number before it.

The Richter scale doesn't measure the amount of damage an earthquake causes. It measures the amount of energy it releases.

▽

MAGNITUDE	EFFECTS	EARTHQUAKES PER YEAR
less than 1.0 to 2.9	not usually felt by people	more than 100,000
3.0 to 3.9	felt by many people; no damage	12,000 to 100,000
4.0 to 4.9	felt by everyone; minor damage	2,000 to 12,000
5.0 to 5.9	some damage to weak buildings	200 to 2,000
6.0 to 6.9	increased damage to populated areas	20 to 200
7.0 to 7.9	serious damage over large areas; loss of life	3 to 20
8.0 and higher	severe damage and loss of life over large areas	fewer than 3

7.3 magnitude earthquake, Taiwan (1993)

An earthquake struck Los Angeles, California, in January 1994. It measured 6.7 magnitude on the Richter scale.

Earthquakes, especially the stronger ones, often occur in series. The earthquake with the greatest magnitude in the series is called the mainshock. A small earthquake is sometimes a sign that a stronger one will follow. An earthquake that comes before the mainshock is called a foreshock.

Strong earthquakes are commonly followed by many earthquakes of lesser magnitude. These are called aftershocks. Aftershocks are the result of Earth's crust settling into place. Each aftershock is less powerful than the one that came before it. However, aftershocks can be as dangerous as the mainshock and can contribute to damage.

Man-Made Earthquakes

Not all earthquakes are caused by natural processes. Some are caused by people. Mining and drilling projects deep underground can weaken Earth's crust and make it crack and slip. The weight of man-made lakes behind large dams can set off earthquakes. Militaries have also caused earthquakes by testing **nuclear** weapons underground.

dam with flood gates

THE EFFECTS OF EARTHQUAKES

Strong earthquakes that strike populated areas cause great destruction. Buildings, bridges, and other structures break and fall. People are harmed and sometimes trapped by falling **debris**. Tremors may also destroy roads and railroads. The ground may even crack open and seem to swallow cars and buildings!

Earthquakes can create landslides. The moving masses of rock and earth can cover or even destroy homes, roads, and other structures. Strong earthquakes at sea cause giant waves called tsunamis. When tsunamis hit land, they flood cities and towns, knock down structures, and drown people. Severe tremors can make soil loose, causing structures to topple.

Indian Ocean Tsunami, 2004

On December 26, 2004, a 9.1 magnitude earthquake on the bottom of the Indian Ocean created a tsunami. Giant waves hammered 11 countries. The island of Sumatra got hit the worst. Waves traveled as far as 3,000 miles (4,800 km), striking Africa. More than 200,000 people died, making it the deadliest tsunami on record.

5.1 magnitude earthquake, Spain (2011)

An Indonesian man walks among the debris
following the Indian Ocean tsunami of 2004.

SAN FRANCISCO 1906

The deadliest earthquake in US history occurred near the city of San Francisco in 1906. The earthquake was the result of movement in the San Andreas fault. After just 60 seconds of tremors, San Francisco—as well as other parts of California—experienced incredible amounts of damage. Altogether, more than 28,000 buildings were destroyed. Out of a population of about 400,000, about 225,000 people were left homeless. The earthquake started fires that swept through the city for 3 days.

About 3,000 people died as a result of the 1906 earthquake. Shortly after, scientists began studying the San Andreas fault. This marked the beginning of modern earthquake study in the United States.

view of street following San Francisco earthquake of 1906

The 1906 San Francisco earthquake was recorded by seismographs as far away as Germany.

▽

The Alaskan Tsunami

On March 27, 1964, a 9.2 magnitude earthquake struck Prince William Sound near Alaska. It was the largest recorded earthquake in North America. The quake created a tsunami that hit land from Alaska south through California. Whole coastal communities were wiped out in Alaska, and 119 people died.

Anchorage, Alaska (March 1964)

HAITI 2010

On January 12, 2010, a 7.0 magnitude earthquake struck just 25 miles (40 km) west of Port-au-Prince, Haiti. The focus wasn't very deep. It was just 8.1 miles (13 km) beneath Earth's surface, which increased the damage it caused. Over the next several weeks, many aftershocks occurred. Fifty-nine aftershocks were greater than 4.5 on the Richter scale. Two of them were 5.9 and 6.0 in magnitude.

Poor building standards in Haiti resulted in massive damage. Buildings crumbled, trapping and killing many people. Over 200,000 buildings were damaged or destroyed. More than 220,000 people died, 300,000 were injured, and 1.3 million people were left homeless.

The Léogâne Fault

The 2010 Haiti earthquake was caused by a previously unknown fault. Scientists call it the Léogâne fault after a Haitian town directly over it. The fracture is a type of reverse fault known as a thrust fault. One block of Earth's crust moves up and over another block.

Port-au-Prince, Haiti (January 2010)

Rescuers from around the world flew into Port-au-Prince following the 2010 quake. Despite the continuing efforts to clear the rubble and rebuild, much of the country still needs help today.

23

JAPAN 2011

On March 11, 2011, a 9.0 magnitude earthquake occurred off the northeastern coast of Japan. It was the most destructive earthquake in the country's history. Several foreshocks struck in the days before the mainshock, and hundreds of aftershocks followed. Soon after the earthquake, a tsunami hit the coast. Together, the earthquake and the tsunami killed more than 14,000 people. Seven weeks after the disaster, 13,000 people were still missing.

The tsunami struck the Fukushima Daiichi Nuclear Power Station, which suffered major damage. The power station caught on fire, and **radioactive** fuel leaked into the ocean and air.

Fukushima Daiichi Nuclear Power Station (March 2011)

The Hero Mayor

One Japanese town escaped the tsunami's effects, thanks to a past leader. Kotaku Wamura, former mayor of Fudai, saw a tsunami destroy his town in 1933. Although many people thought he was crazy, Wamura had a large wall built to protect the town when he was mayor. Today, the people of Fudai are grateful for his efforts.

◄ This photo shows the debris left after a tsunami struck the coast of Japan in 2011. Houses and debris are piled on top of a bridge.

25

PREDICTING EARTHQUAKES

After years of studying earthquakes, scientists still can't predict when and where they'll occur. However, they can predict where one is likely to occur based on previous earthquakes, the movement of plates, and the positions of fault lines.

Scientists can also give a general idea of when a quake might occur. If an area has had a history of earthquakes, perhaps one every 200 years, scientists will say it's probable one will occur again in the next 50 to 100 years. In the end, predictions can't give us an exact idea of where and when an earthquake may happen.

Can Animals Predict Earthquakes?

Throughout history, there have been reports of animals acting strangely before earthquakes. Ancient Greek historians recorded that rats, snakes, and weasels fled the city of Helice days before an earthquake struck. Recent stories suggest that the common toad can predict earthquakes, too. How do they do it? We may never know!

A seismologist points to a seismograph's reading of a 6.0 magnitude earthquake that struck Portugal in 2007.

earthquake watch station, New York City

PREPARED AND SAFE

Since the 1906 San Francisco quake, earthquake preparations have advanced. Structures built where earthquakes commonly occur are stronger than they once were. Some are even built to sway during a quake instead of break.

If you live where earthquakes occur, there's a lot you and your family can do to be prepared for a quake. Keep an emergency kit with drinking water, food, flashlights, fire extinguishers, and first aid supplies in your home. Know how to shut off gas, electricity, and water in case the lines break. Secure refrigerators and water heaters to walls to stop them from falling over. Store breakables on low shelves. Practice how to stay safe during an earthquake.

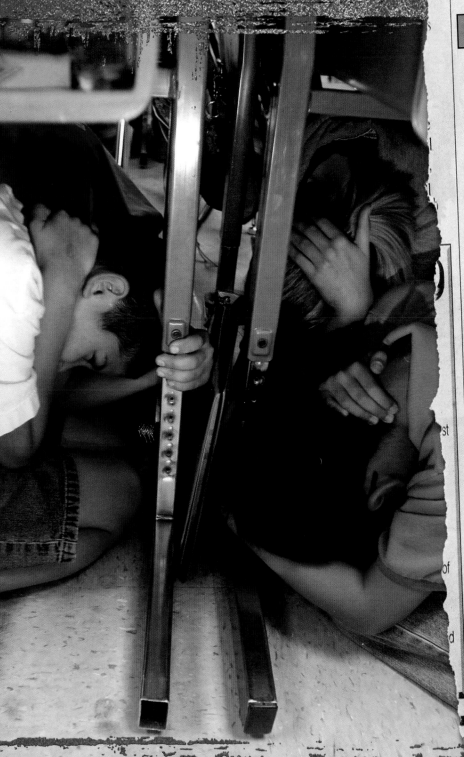

Earthquake Safety

If you're indoors:
- hide under a heavy table or desk
- stay away from windows
- stay away from walls that may fall
- don't use elevators
- don't run outside or you might get hit by falling debris

If you're outside:
- run to an open area away from buildings, trees, and power lines
- don't run into a building

If you're in a car:
- stop as quickly and safely as you can
- stay in the car
- steer clear of buildings, trees, power lines, and bridges

▲
These students practice what to do if an earthquake strikes while they're in school.

GLOSSARY

calculate: to figure something out using math

damage: harm. Also, to cause harm.

debris: pieces of something that has been destroyed or broken

destruction: the state of being destroyed or ruined

geologist: a scientist who studies Earth and its history

horizontally: going from side to side

landslide: the sudden movement of rock and dirt down a hill or mountain

magnitude: a measure of the power of an earthquake

nuclear: having to do with the power created by splitting atoms, the smallest pieces of matter

predict: to guess what will happen in the future based on facts or knowledge

radioactive: giving off a harmful kind of energy

reverse: opposite to what is usual or normal

topple: to fall forward or tip over

tremor: a shaking movement caused by an earthquake

FOR MORE INFORMATION

Books

Fradin, Judy, and Dennis Fradin. *Witness to Disaster: Earthquakes.* Washington, DC: National Geographic, 2008.

Rooney, Anne. *Earthquake!* North Mankato, MN: Arcturus Publishing, 2006.

Yep, Laurence. *The Earth Dragon Awakes: The San Francisco Earthquake of 1906.* New York, NY: HarperCollins Publishers, 2006.

Websites

Earthquakes
www.fema.gov/kids/quake.htm
Read about historic earthquakes, and complete activities to learn more about them.

Earthquakes for Kids
earthquake.usgs.gov/learn/kids/
Find out where and when the most recent earthquakes occurred, and read about earthquake safety.

INDEX